THE LEGACY OF THE ANCIENT WORLD

THE NEAR EAST

MIKE CORBISHLEY

MACDONALD YOUNG BOOKS

First published in 1995 by Macdonald Young Books
Campus 400
Maylands Avenue
Hemel Hempstead
Hertfordshire HP2 7EZ
Originally published in 1994 as part of the title *Pathways,
Timelines of the Ancient World*

A CIP catalogue for this book is available from the
British Library

ISBN 0 7500 1808 9

Commissioning Editor: Thomas Keegan
Editors: Jill A. Laidlaw, Smantha Armstrong
Designer: Simon Borrough
Picture Researcher: Juliet Duff
Illustrators: Swanston Publishing Ltd., Jonathan Potter,
Steve Roberts, Deborah Kindred (Simon Girling & Associates)
Adrian Barclay, Lee Montgomery (Beehive Illustration)

Text copyright © 1994 Mike Corbishley
Illustrations copyright © 1994 Macdonald Young Books

Printed in Portugal

Cover illustration: Swanston Publishing Ltd.

Cover photographs: Michael Holford: left. **The Bridgeman
Art Library**: right.

Map artwork: Swanston Publishing Ltd.

Picture Acknowledgements
The author and publisher would like to acknowledge, with
thanks, the following photographic sources:

Ancient Art & Architecture Collection: 13 left, 25. **Michael
Holford**: 13 centre, 20, 21, 23, 26. **Werner Forman
Archive**: 17.

CONTENTS

Words in **bold** are explained in the glossary on page 28.

INTRODUCTION

Today it is possible to travel thousands of kilometres by air from one continent to another in just a few hours. The world seems like a small place because images of people from far-off countries are beamed into our front rooms on to our television sets. In ancient times, travel was difficult and slow — many parts of the world would have been far too dangerous for strangers. Even today, people without modern technology, such as jet travel and television, often know little about the lands and the peoples beyond their own countries, or even beyond their own villages.

Despite these difficulties, there were connections between ancient peoples thousands of years ago. *The Legacy of the Ancient World* tells the stories of some of those connections. This book talks about some of the most important peoples of the Near East.

The Near East

This book starts with the world's earliest civilization, Sumeria, which was in the Near East. Sumeria was famous for a number of important inventions such as writing and the wheel, and it was also where the world's first cities were built.

Egypt, Israel and Islam

The first ever recorded sea voyage was made from Egypt around 3200 BC. Egyptian hieroglyphs give us the details of this adventure. The pages on Egypt show us that the ancient Egyptians did not like travelling themselves, yet their merchants journeyed into Africa and across the Mediterranean Sea. Two of the world's main religions, Judaism and Christianity, began in Israel and another great religion, Islam began in the Middle East.

Throughout *The Legacy of the Ancient World* you will find Time Lines (below). The key dates and events listed in the Time Lines will help you to see what is happening in each civilization. You will be able to relate these dates to some of the things happening in other places all over the world.

SUMERIA

BC
c. 9000 Wheat crops
        cultivated in Syria
        Sheep domesticated in
        Mesopotamia
c. 7000 Çatal Hüyük founded
c. 6000 Farming established in
        Mesopotamia
c. 4500 Boats with sails in use in
        Mesopotamia

THE WORLD

BC
c. 8500 First rock art in the Sahara
        region
        First cultivation of wild
        grasses in Peru
c. 8300 Glaciers retreat in Europe
c. 7000 First crops cultivated in
        Mexico and in New Guinea
c. 6500 Britain separates from
        Europe

Dates are given in the usual way — BC and AD. AD is an abbreviation of two **Latin** words *Anno Domini*. Latin was the language used by the Romans. These two words mean "in the year of the lord". This was the system of dating invented by the Christians. Dates are counted from the birth of Jesus Christ. This system of dating is used in most parts of the world today. For example, the first astronauts to step on to the surface of the moon did so on in July AD 1969 — but this date is usually just written as 1969. Dates before the birth of Christ are counted backwards and have the letters BC after them. For example, the Roman general, Julius Caesar, first invaded Britain in 55 BC and then in the following year, 54 BC.

Sometimes we do not know precise dates for something that happened a very long time ago. You will see the letter c. used before dates like these. It is also an abbreviation of a Latin word, *circa*, which means 'about'.

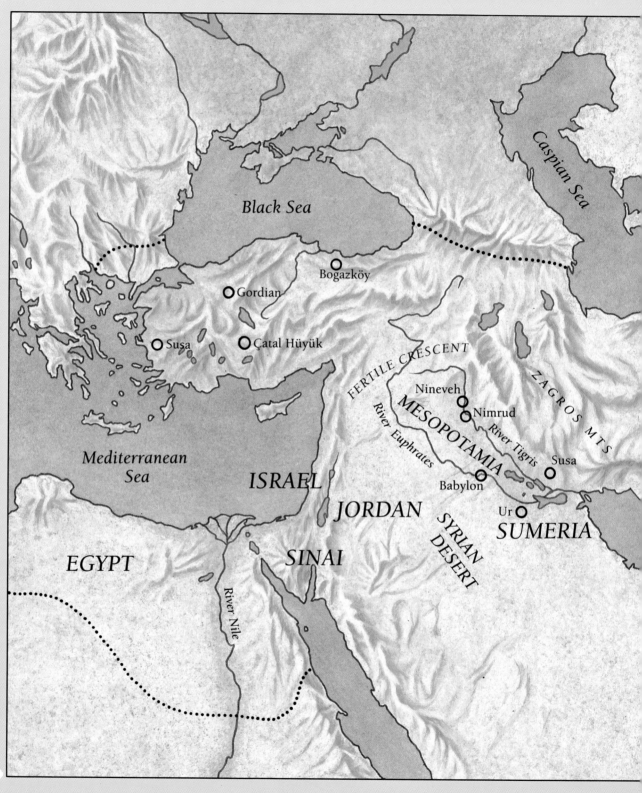

THE WHEAT WE EAT
Eleven thousand years ago, **hunter-gatherer** people discovered how to tame wild animals and **cultivate** crops. These crops, called emmer and einkorn, are the wild ancestors of the wheat we eat today. These crops were first cultivated in the area known as the Fertile Crescent, the lands between the Zagros Mountains of Iran and southern Israel and Jordan.

HUNTERS AND FARMERS
The hunters of the Fertile Crescent herded gazelles and wild goats. Gradually they began to tame (domesticate) the goats and breed them for food. Other animals, such as sheep, became farm animals in Mesopotamia around 9000 BC, pigs around 7000 BC in Turkey, and cattle around 6000 BC in northern Africa and the lands around the Aegean Sea.

THE PERSIANS
King Darius I (c. 522–486 BC) reorganized the territory of the Persians and by around 500 BC he controlled the largest empire the world had ever seen. Darius began building a new capital city, called Persepolis.
See pages 16–17.

ÇATAL HÜYÜK
Çatal Hüyük, in Turkey, was one of the largest farming villages in the Near East. By about 7000 BC, wheat and barley were being grown and pigs bred as farm animals. By about 6000 BC Çatal Hüyük was a town with a population of around 6,000 people.

Caspian Sea

Black Sea

Bogazköy

Gordian

Susa

Çatal Hüyük

FERTILE CRESCENT

Nineveh

Nimrud

MESOPOTAMIA

River Euphrates

River Tigris

ZAGROS MTS

Susa

Babylon

Mediterranean Sea

ISRAEL

JORDAN

SYRIAN DESERT

Ur

SUMERIA

EGYPT

SINAI

River Nile

WRITING WITH PICTURES
Around 3200 BC the Sumerian people invented writing in the form of pictures. Each little drawing represented something — usually trading goods or possessions.
See page 11.

WRITING ON WET CLAY
Sumerian pictogram writing developed into the writing we call cuneiform. Cuneiform means 'wedge-shaped writing'. Clerks used pens made of reed to push the wedge shapes into wet clay to form individual words.
See page 11.

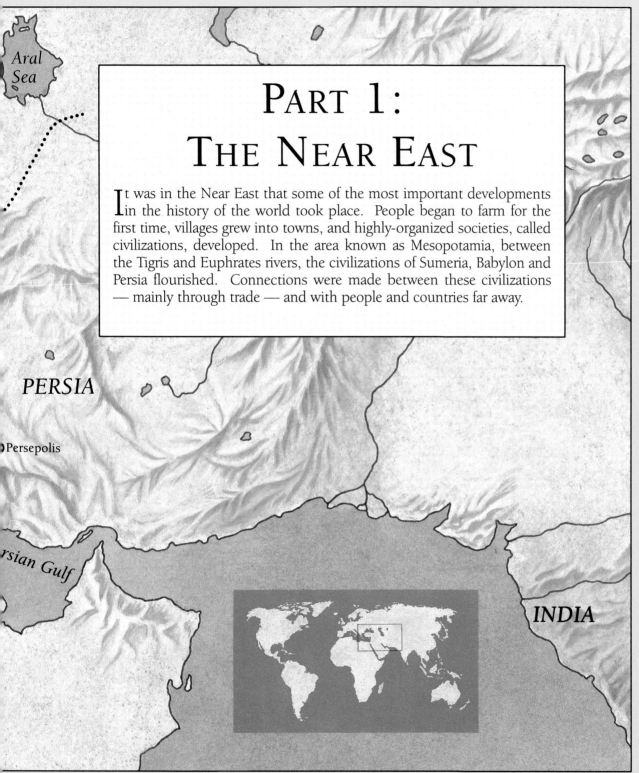

THE HANGING GARDENS OF BABYLON
One of the **Seven Wonders of the Ancient World** was the Hanging Gardens of Babylon. These beautiful terraced gardens, built like the architecture of a ziggurat, were said to have been built by King Nebuchadnezzar II (king of Babylon from 604 BC) for his wife Amityia, to remind her of the cool green mountain area she had come from. See page 14.

GOLD AND SILVER
Persian rulers and nobles were extremely wealthy. They employed craftworkers to make beautiful objects. Turn to page 16 to see a Persian drinking horn from the fifth century BC.

THE ISHTAR GATE
The huge city of Babylon was surrounded by walls and great gateways. Each gate was dedicated to one of their gods. Turn to page 15 to see a reconstruction of the Ishtar Gate, dedicated to the Babylonian goddess of love, Ishtar.

PART 1:
THE NEAR EAST

It was in the Near East that some of the most important developments in the history of the world took place. People began to farm for the first time, villages grew into towns, and highly-organized societies, called civilizations, developed. In the area known as Mesopotamia, between the Tigris and Euphrates rivers, the civilizations of Sumeria, Babylon and Persia flourished. Connections were made between these civilizations — mainly through trade — and with people and countries far away.

Aral Sea

PERSIA

Persepolis

Persian Gulf

INDIA

ASSYRIA
With their great armies, the **Assyrian** kings took over the kingdom of Ur in Babylonia, conquered Egypt, and controlled the eastern part of the Mediterranean Sea. The Assyrian capitals Nimrud and Nineveh were destroyed in 612 BC

ZIGGURATS
One important feature of Sumerian cities was the ziggurat — a temple tower. Ziggurats sometimes stood inside a walled **sacred** enclosure in the centre of the city. See pages 12–13 for the Ziggurat built for the moon god Nanna in the city of Ur.

THE HITTITES
The Hittites were another of the peoples who tried to dominate the Near East. Over a period of 400 years they created an empire that even challenged the power of the Egyptians. Their powerful armies used horses and chariots. Their capital was at a place now called Bogazköy in modern-day Turkey.

BC
c. 9000 Wheat crops
cultivated in Syria
Sheep domesticated in
Mesopotamia
c. 7000 Catal Hüyük founded
c. 6000 Farming established in
Mesopotamia
c. 4500 Boats with sails in use in
Mesopotamia

SUMERIA

c. 3500 First cities in Sumeria
c. 3200 Earliest writing in the
world in Sumeria
The wheel is invented
c. 3100 Cuneiform writing in
Sumeria
Long-distance trade with
Syria
c. 2500 City-states such as Ur
in Sumeria

The world's first cities were built around 5,000 years ago in the country now called Iraq. This was the land of Sumeria (also called Mesopotamia). The land was very **fertile** and most of the people who lived in the cities were farmers. The first farming villages in the region were in northern Sumeria. By about 5500 BC wealthy farming communities were building villages which later became small towns further south nearer the Persian Gulf.

Sumeria was very organized. From the records and buildings that have been **excavated** we can identify priests, rulers, craftworkers, traders and **administrators**.

TRADE

As the Sumerians became better farmers they found that they had more food than they needed. They could trade their extra crops and **import** goods which they were unable to grow or make themselves. The rivers and the sea became major highways. The ship above is a typical Mesopotamian trading boat.

There were two harbours inside the walls of the capital city of Ur so that traders could reach the sea by the River Euphrates. The goods the traders of Sumeria imported included gold from Egypt, lapis lazuli (a bright, blue stone used in jewellery making) from Afghanistan, tin from around the Caspian Sea, timber from the coast of the Mediterranean and copper from India.

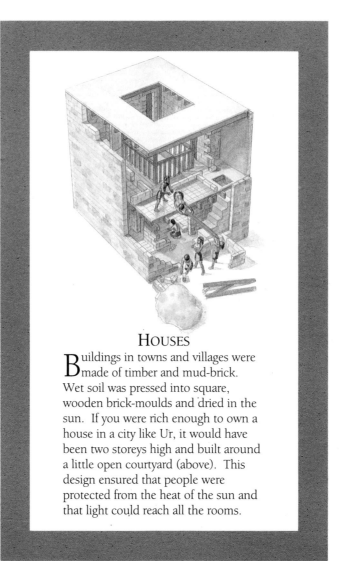

HOUSES

Buildings in towns and villages were made of timber and mud-brick. Wet soil was pressed into square, wooden brick-moulds and dried in the sun. If you were rich enough to own a house in a city like Ur, it would have been two storeys high and built around a little open courtyard (above). This design ensured that people were protected from the heat of the sun and that light could reach all the rooms.

AGRICULTURE

In northern Sumeria, farmers could rely on plenty of rain to help them grow their crops (above) and feed their animals. But in the south, where the first large cities were built, there was not enough rain for farming. The Sumerians had to **irrigate** their fields by digging canals to carry water from the spring flooding of the Tigris and Euphrates rivers.

10

BC
c. 8500 First rock art in the Sahara region
First cultivation of wild grasses in Peru
c. 8300 Glaciers retreat in Europe
c. 7000 First crops cultivated in Mexico and in New Guinea
c. 6500 Britain separates from Europe

THEIR LEGACIES

The people of Sumeria were the first to organize their society on a grand scale and to build large cities. They were also responsible for a number of important inventions. The earliest evidence for the wheel comes from Sumeria. The Sumerians invented writing (cuneiform) and a mathematical system based on the number 60. They divided the hour into 60 minutes and the circle into 360 degrees. By observing the moon they worked out the lunar calendar that we still use today.

c. 6000 First farming villages in China
c. 4500 Farming around the River Ganges in India
c. 3500 Simple ploughs first used in northern and western Europe
c. 3000 Egyptian hieroglyphic writing

UR

The city of Ur (above) is famous for its royal tombs and palaces. The city was important around 2500 BC when it had a population of around 20,000 people.

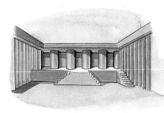

URUK

Mesopotamia was made up of independent states, called city-states. Each city-state's boundaries were based on the land around a city. One of the most important states was Uruk which was built on a river that ran into the River Euphrates. Uruk grew until its walls ran around 450 **hectares** of land and it had a population of about 50,000 people. In the centre of this great city was a sacred complex of temples. The Cone Mosaic Court above was part of this complex.

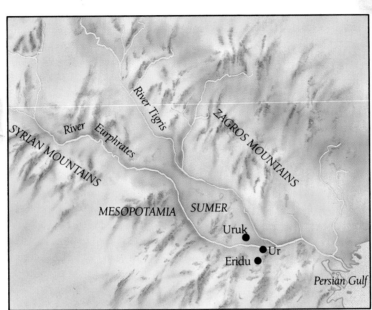

ERIDU

Eridu (above) was the most southerly city of Sumeria and probably the oldest — beginning around 5000 BC. It grew into a large and important city.
Archaeologists have excavated two palaces of the kings of Uruk and a ziggurat (see following two pages). The city of Eridu became less important as Ur became more powerful.

WRITING

The earliest Sumerian writing looked like pictures of the goods or property that people wanted to keep a record of. These images are called pictograms. Sumerian pictograms were developed into a form of writing called cuneiform. To write in cuneiform you had to press a wedge into wet clay and then bake the clay. Each pictogram became a symbol.

 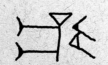 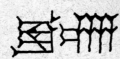

THE CITY OF UR

Ur was originally a small settlement in southern Sumeria around 4500 BC. The settlement grew into a city and its most important period began around 2100 BC under King Ur-Nammu. He ordered a defensive wall to be constructed around the city. The city was also defended by water — the River Euphrates ran along one side of the city and a canal was dug around the remaining city limits. Two harbours provided protection and docks for the ships of the city's traders.

Towering above the city, visible to everyone, was the temple tower, called a ziggurat. It was built to provide a temple to the Sumerian moon god, called Nanna. In the centre of the city were royal palaces and the tombs of previous kings. In this Royal **mausoleum** the kings and queens of Ur, and their servants, were buried. The houses, shops and workshops of Ur's inhabitants filled the city walls and spread out far beyond into the suburbs.

BC

c. 3500 Llama first used as a pack animal in Peru
First farmers in the Indus Valley

c. 3000 First evidence of Egyptian hieroglyphic writing

c. 2600 Temple mounds and religious centres in Peru

THEIR ACHIEVEMENTS

The greatest achievement of the people of Sumeria was to establish a society based on cities. Very large numbers of people could be fed by the food grown on the fertile land of Mesopotamia. Not everyone had to be a farmer because food was plentiful. Other workers exchanged their labour or the products they made for food.

c. 2500 First wheel-thrown pottery in China
Sahara begins to dry out

c. 2000 Inuits (Eskimos) reach northern part of Greenland
Agriculture in New Guinea

This head came from a marble statue. It is thought to be King Sargon I who took control of the city-states of Sumeria and ruled the region as one country from around 2300 BC. His capital, Agade, has not yet been discovered.

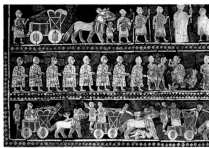

This beautifully decorated object is a sounding box for a musical instrument. It was found in a royal tomb. This side of the box shows scenes of the king in battle with his soldiers, chariots and prisoners of war. The other side of the box shows the king at a banquet.

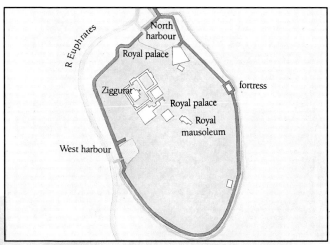

You can see a plan of the city of Ur above and a reconstruction of the city below.

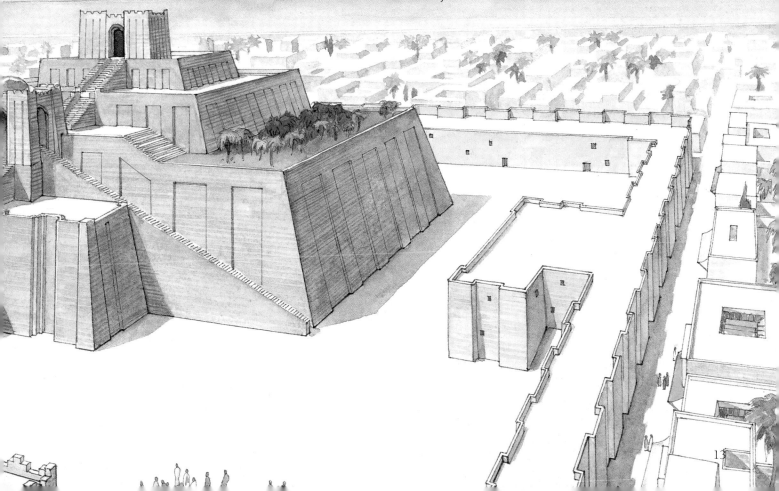

BABYLON

BC
2340	King Sargon I ruled from city of Agade
2330	City-states around Agade united by King Sargon
2150	Agade invaded by people of Iran
c. 2050	Warfare between Sumerian states
c. 2000	Amorite dynasties rule Babylonia

1800	Assyrians invade northern Babylonia. Assyria established as an empire
1792– 1750	King Hammurabi rules Babylon
625- 539	New Babylonian Empire established
604– 562	Reign of Nebuchadnezzar II rebuilds and enlarges Babylon

The Assyrian Empire (c. 1200 BC) flourished long after cities like Ur controlled Mesopotamia. This empire later fell to other powerful peoples. King Nabopolassar defeated the Assyrians and established a new Babylonian Empire in 625 BC. His son, Nebuchadnezzar, controlled a huge empire which stretched from the Persian Gulf to the Mediterranean Sea. He even fought off an invasion by the Egyptians (see pages 20–23).

King Nebuchadnezzar rebuilt the capital city, Babylon, putting up huge public buildings, temples, ziggurats and a palace. The city was defended by a canal linked to the River Euphrates which ran through the city. Double defensive walls were built around the city with nine impressive gateways. But, in 539 BC, Babylon was captured by King Cyrus of Persia. A new civilization had come to Mesopotamia.

The Hanging Gardens of Babylon seemed marvellous to the travellers who came to the city. These terraced gardens brought greenery and water into a hot and dusty city.

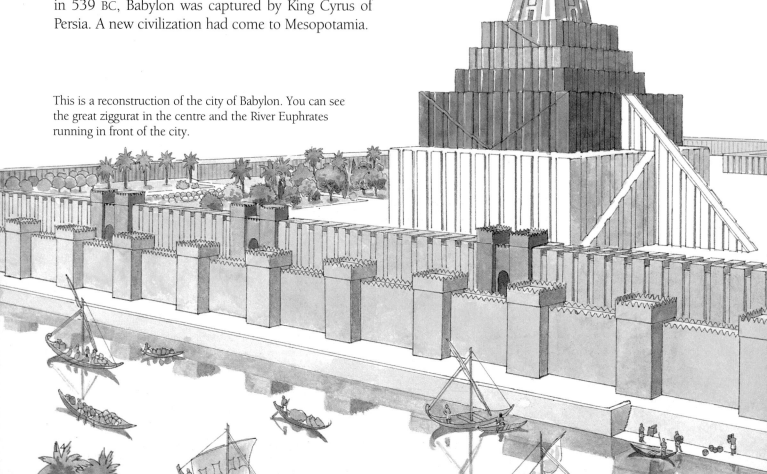

This is a reconstruction of the city of Babylon. You can see the great ziggurat in the centre and the River Euphrates running in front of the city.

14

BC
c. 2300 Settlements in Mesoamerica
2205   China's first emperor, Yu
c. 2000 Inuits (Eskimos) reach
         northern part of Greenland
         Palaces built on Crete
c. 1500 Mycenaean civilization
         established
         Aryan peoples invade
         northern India
c. 1000 People reach almost all the
         Polynesian islands
         Phoenician alphabet
         introduced

The Babylonians used the Sumerians' inventions and developed their sciences of astronomy, mathematics and medicine even further. They watched the heavens carefully and were able to make accurate predictions about the year based on the movements of the sun and the moon. In the Babylonian city of Kish, the records which have been discovered of the movements of the planet Venus are so accurate that we can work out precise dates for the early kings of Mesopotamia by matching them with modern astronomical records.

Eastern Woodland peoples
of North America build
burial mounds
David anointed King of
Israel
c. 900– Etruscan cities established
800
753   Traditional date for the
         foundation of Rome

King Hammurabi (1792–1750 BC) founded the first capital of Babylonia at Babylon. It replaced the original Mesopotamian capital of Ur. Hammurabi was famous for making nearly 300 laws for his people. One of the most famous laws said: *'If a citizen has put out a citizen's eye, they shall put out his eye. If a citizen has broken a citizen's bone, they shall break his bone.'* The same idea of justice can be seen in the *Old Testament* of the *Bible* (see page 25) in the phrase, *'an eye for an eye, a tooth for a tooth'*.

GOVERNING AN EMPIRE

Another of Hammurabi's laws said: *'If a citizen hired an ox and caused its death through carelessness or through beating, he shall replace an ox with an ox for the owner'*.

The kings of Mesopotamia used stones to mark the limits of their territory (below). Boundary stones were also used to record grants of land to owners.

The Ishtar Gate (below) was decorated with blue and gold bricks.

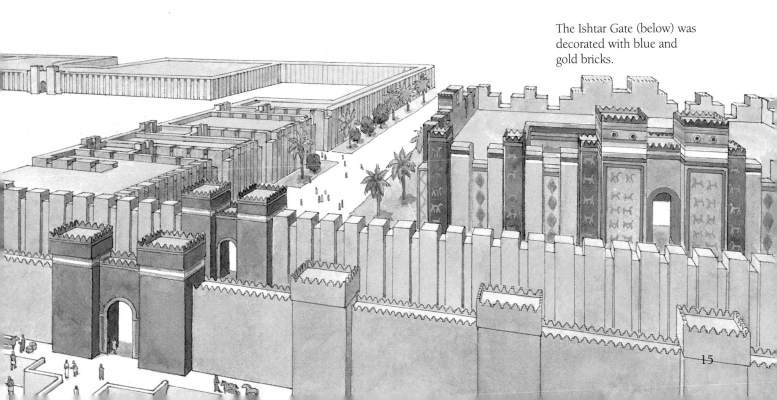

PERSIA

Great civilizations and empires occupied the land of Sumeria, Assyria and Babylonia. To the east were a number of **nomadic** peoples who had travelled west from Central Asia. Two of these peoples, the Medes and the Persians, were united under the Persian king Cyrus II, the Great. He began to conquer many lands to create an empire and, in 539 BC, captured the city of Babylon itself.

The next Persian king, Darius I, reorganized the empire and made new conquests. He fought with the Greeks and by around 500 BC he controlled the largest empire the world had ever seen. Darius set up areas, called *satrapies*, which were governed by Persians loyal to him. A reconstruction of a satrapy governor's house can be seen below.

Persian rulers and nobles were extremely wealthy. They employed craftworkers to make beautiful objects like this drinking horn.

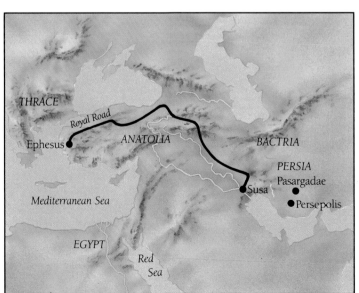

EPHESUS
Ephesus, on the western edge of the Persian Empire, was a major city standing at one end of the Royal Road. The road, which started at Susa, was constructed so that royal **couriers** could travel quickly from one end of the empire to the other. A courier could travel the 2,700 kilometres of the Royal Road in a week.

PERSEPOLIS
King Darius decided to build a palace worthy of the greatness of his empire. He chose a site 480 kilometres south-east of Susa at a place to be known as Persepolis. Building began in about 520 BC and was not finished for 60 years, long after Darius' death. Skilled workers came from all over the empire. Some of the best stonemasons probably travelled from Greece.

THE WORLD

BC
509 Last Etruscan king,
     Tarquinius Superbus
     (Tarquin the Proud),
     expelled by the Romans
c. 500 Cast iron first used in China
        Wet rice cultivated in Japan
        Villages of hunters and
        fishers in Alaska
490 Greeks revolt against
     Persians and defeat them at
     the Battle of Marathon

THEIR ACHIEVEMENTS

*The king of the Persians, Darius I, knew how to rule and control his huge territory. The idea of building an efficient road system was something many other emperors and dictators copied later. Darius knew that he needed to have detailed information about his empire if he was going to control it properly. He had a **survey** carried out of all the land in the empire to decide what taxes people could afford to pay.*

447 Parthenon begun in Athens
c. 400 Olmec civilization in decline
        in Mesoamerica
390 Celts sack city of Rome
379 Chinese philosopher
     Confucius dies
c. 370 Nazca peoples settle in
        villages in Peru
327 Alexander the Great begins
     campaigns in India

A stairway in Persepolis built during the time of Xerxes I in the first half of the fifth century BC.

THE RIVER NILE

The farming land of ancient Egypt was 'the gift of the Nile' according to the Greek historian, **Herodotus**. The Egyptians called their country the 'Black Land' because each year the River Nile flooded and carried black mud on to the surrounding fields. The silt made the land very fertile and it could support crops, animals and birds.

BOATS ON THE NILE

The boat was the most important form of transport and the Nile was Egypt's main highway. The earliest Egyptian boats were made of bundles of papyrus stalks tied together. These boats were propelled by paddles or poles. Sea-going ships were given grand names such as Star of Memphis. Egyptian boats sailed from the Nile to the Red Sea, over the Mediterranean and to **Nubia**.

THE BIBLE

In the land of Israel the Hebrews worshipped one god, whom they called Yahweh. The sacred book of this religion and their history was in fact a collection of books which became known as the Old Testament of the Bible. It is from the Bible that we have evidence of the 12 tribes of Israel. See page 24.

SOLOMON'S TEMPLE

The Israelite king, Solomon (966–926 BC), built a splendid temple to Yahweh in Jerusalem. The most sacred object of the Hebrew religion (later known as Judaism) — the Ark of the Covenant — was kept in the Temple. See page 25.

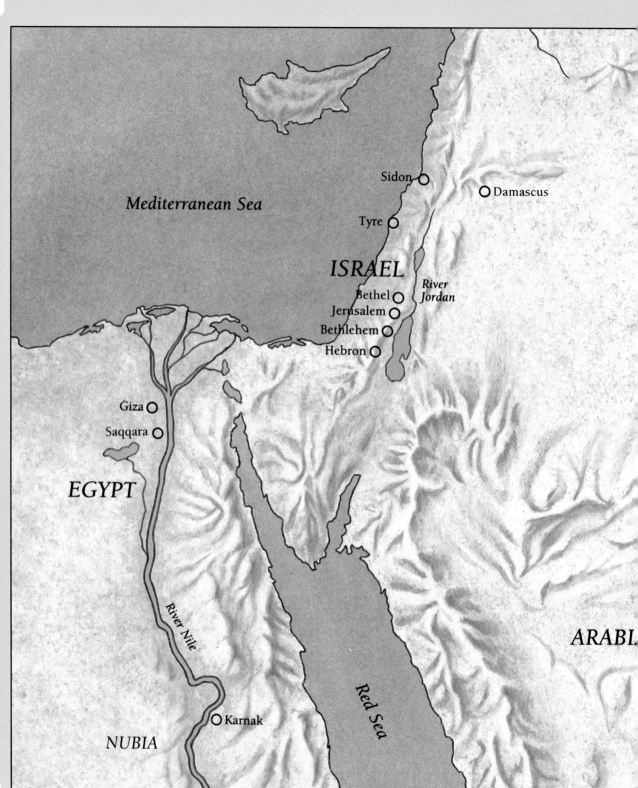

PEOPLE FROM THE SEA

The Egyptians wrote about enemies who 'came out of the sea'. We do not know where these sea peoples came from but we do know that they launched attacks on Egypt and other countries. Some settled as **mercenary** soldiers in Egypt, others, known as the Peleset, gave their name to the land of Palestine.

THE PHOENICIAN ALPHABET

By 1000 BC the Phoenicians developed their own alphabet which was made up of only 22 letters. The Greeks expanded this alphabet by adding vowels. The Romans then adapted the Greek version of the alphabet and this alphabet is the basis of the one we use today.

EGYPTIAN MUMMIES

The Egyptians believed in life after death and preserved the bodies of the dead to help them live for ever. Experts prepared the body for mummification in a process which often took 70 days (see page 23). Bodies were wrapped and put inside elaborately carved and painted coffins.

SACRED ANIMALS

The Egyptians kept pet monkeys and gazelles, but some animals were thought to be sacred. They worshipped the cat goddess, Bastet, and held a special festival once a year in her honour. Cats were also mummified when they died — as were several other animals. Mummified dogs, snakes, birds and fish have been found.

PART 2: EGYPT, ISRAEL AND ISLAM

One of the most important civilizations in the ancient world was created by the Egyptians. They became wealthy and very powerful and influenced many peoples. The ancient Egyptians were responsible for some of the world's most extraordinary buildings — the pyramids. The following pages also look at some of the peoples of the eastern coasts of the Mediterranean Sea who began to establish their civilizations around 1000 BC.

KING TUTANKHAMUN

One of the most famous archaeological discoveries ever made was the tomb of King Tutankhamun (c. 1361–1339 BC). The tomb was undisturbed by tomb robbers and was discovered in 1922. The king had been buried with rooms full of marvellous objects such as model boats, boxes, board games, food and jewellery. These objects give us a detailed picture of life in the royal court around 1340 BC. See page 21.

PAPYRUS

The ancient Egyptians invented a sort of paper which continued to be used even in Roman times (after 30 BC). It was made from the stalk of a river plant called the papyrus. Read page 20 to discover how papyrus paper was made.

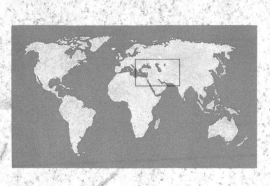

Persian Gulf

THE PHOENICIANS

Around 1200 BC people called the Phoenicians began to take over the sea trade of the eastern Mediterranean. They were great sea-faring traders and warriors. The Phoenicians established their own cities and, in Roman times, became known as the Carthaginians because their biggest city was Carthage, in north Africa.

EGYPTIAN WRITING

The Egyptians invented their own form of writing which we call hieroglyphic. Like cuneiform (see page 11), hieroglyphs were made up from pictograms. There were also signs for numbers. See page 20.

c. 4000	Larger farming villages in Egypt
	Boats with sails in use on the River Nile
3050	Foundation of the Egyptian state
	First pharaoh is called Narmer

EGYPT

c. 3000	Egyptian hieroglyphics
2920	Menes becomes the first pharaoh of a unified Egypt
	Trade with Mesopotamia
c. 2630	First pyramid begun
c. 2600	First 'true' pyramid begun
c. 2550	Great Pyramid built at Giza

The first people who lived in the valley of the River Nile hunted and fished for food. Each year the Nile flooded and washed a layer of mud on to the surrounding land. This mud was full of **nutrients** which fed the land, which in turn fed crops and animals. Hunters became farmers because the land was so fertile.

The wealthy kingdom of Egypt thrived between 3100 and 332 BC. Egypt was originally divided into two parts — Lower Egypt and Upper Egypt. Each part was governed by one king. But in about 2920 BC the whole of Egypt became one kingdom, with a single king. Much later this king took the grand title of Pharaoh, which meant 'The Great House'. The pharaoh ruled his people with absolute power, as if he were a god. But the pharaoh needed thousands of people to help him run the country. These officials, called **civil servants**, organized big building projects, collected taxes and kept records.

The Egyptians did not rule a very large empire, but their wealth and trading connections meant that other nations owed **allegiance** to the pharaoh. Eventually Egypt was invaded by the Persians, Greeks and Romans, but many aspects of Egyptian life were adopted by the invading peoples.

This model of a boat was found in a rich man's tomb. It dates from 1800 BC.

TRADE

Egyptians did not think much of other countries. They preferred not to travel abroad but their merchants traded with many countries. The Egyptians grew plenty of barley and wheat which could be **exported**. They exchanged their grain for other goods. The land of Nubia, to the south of the kingdom, attracted the Egyptians because there were gold reserves there, as well as precious stones. A very hard black wood, called ebony, was also brought back from Nubia and used for carving ornaments and furniture. Ivory, from elephants' tusks, was a favourite material for carving. Animals such as monkeys and panthers were also imported from Nubia.

The main Egyptian trade route was the River Nile. Beyond river transport, donkeys carried goods, but camels were hardly used until Roman times. There were different types of boats — from heavy grain barges to sailing boats. Wood from cedar trees grown in the Lebanon was often used to construct the boats.

HIEROGLYPHICS

The Egyptians invented hieroglyphics — writing made up of pictograms. Pictures, some of which you can see below, were painted on to papyrus with a brush and ink or carved into stone. The Egyptians probably used about 700 hieroglyphs.

The Egyptians invented their own 'paper' to write on. The papyrus plant is a reed which grows along the banks of the Nile. The Egyptians removed the **pith** and cut the stem into strips. They laid these strips on top of each other (each layer at right angles to the one below) and beat them flat. The papyrus was left to dry and smoothed flat.

2150	Collapse of Old Kingdom
2040	Middle Kingdom period
	Egypt reunited and ruled from Thebes
	Trade with Syria and Palestine
1652	War between Egypt and Hyksos peoples from Asia
1550	Hyksos peoples driven out of Egypt
1367	New king adopts the name Akhenaten

THEIR ACHIEVEMENTS

The Egyptians became very skilful at surveying and measuring. These skills were needed for great building projects such as the pyramids and for the annual measurement of the Nile floods. A Nilometer was invented and set up on Philae island in Upper Egypt to measure the level of the water. A survey was carried out each year to establish who owned which plots of land. Greek and Roman writers tell us that the Egyptians invented the science of geometry to help them with this work.

1367	New capital of Egypt at Amarna
1339	King Tutankhamun buried
1070	New Kingdom of Egypt ends
671	Assyria conquers Egypt
285	First lighthouse in the world built at Alexandria in Egypt
31	Cleopatra, Queen of Egypt, defeated by the Romans at the Battle of Actium and commits suicide
30	Egypt becomes a Roman province

AGRICULTURE

An Egyptian hymn describes the River Nile as the *'food provider, who creates all that is good'*. The Nile was home to fish and wild game. Huge quantities of grain could be grown after the Nile flooded the land. This photograph is of a painting on papyrus showing Egyptians ploughing and harvesting wheat and **flax** around 1346–1300 BC.

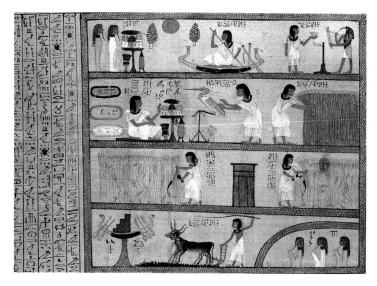

TUTANKHAMUN

The English archaeologist, Howard Carter, caused a world-wide sensation when he discovered the tomb of the boy-king Tutankhamun in the **Valley of the Kings** at Thebes in 1922. Tutankhamun's preserved body was encased in three gold coffins. The gold mask which covered his face is shown above.

SAQQARA

Saqqara was the burial place of the capital of Egypt, Memphis. The Step Pyramid (above) was built for King Djoser.

ABU SIMBEL

Pharaoh Ramesses II, who came to the throne in about 1273 BC, built two temples for himself and his wife on the island of Philae in the Upper Nile, called Abu Simbel (above).

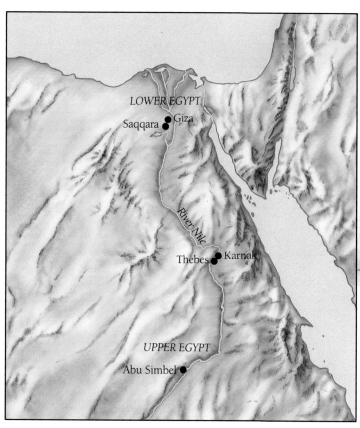

LOWER EGYPT

Saqqara • Giza

River Nile

Thebes • Karnak

UPPER EGYPT

Abu Simbel •

KARNAK

In ancient times Karnak was called Thebes and it was the Egyptian capital from around 1550 BC. Several temples have been excavated there including one to the god Amun (above).

21

THE WORLD

BC
c. 3200 Maize first cultivated in
Mesoamerica
c. 2500 First cities of the Indus
Civilization in India
Sahara begins to dry out
Walled settlements in China
Metal first used in Britain
City-states in Mesopotamia

THEIR LEGACIES

Ancient peoples were fascinated by the Egyptians and their monuments, especially the pyramids. One of the first tourists to visit Egypt was the Greek historian, Herodotus, in the fifth century BC. He brought some of the history and the mystery of Egypt to the West. This century, the discovery of Tutankhamun brought about a new interest in Egyptian styles in architecture, decoration and furniture, which had been popular in nineteenth-century Europe. The calendar of 12 months, which was invented by the Egyptians, was introduced to the West via trade with the Romans.

c. 2000 Inuits (Eskimos) first reach
northern part of Greenland
First settlers in New Guinea
1600 Shang Dynasty in China
1500 Mycenaean civilization
established
c. 1200 First cities in Mesoamerica
Hittite Empire collapses

GODS AND GODDESSES

The sun god Amun-re (1), was shown in different forms with different names. Here (2) he is called Khepri and is shown as a **scarab beetle**. Isis (3) was the goddess of women. She was the wife of Osiris (4) and the mother of Horus (5). Horus, the sky god, is pictured as a falcon. Osiris was the god of the dead and the underworld. He was also seen as responsible for the annual Nile flood and for rebirth after death.

THE PYRAMIDS AT GIZA

At Giza in Lower Egypt was one of the Seven Wonders of the Ancient World — the pyramids. The earliest type of pyramid was the step-pyramid like the one at Saqqara (see page 21). At Giza the pyramids were constructed with smooth sides. The greatest pyramid of all, the Great Pyramid (below), was built as the burial place of King Khufu in about 2550 BC.

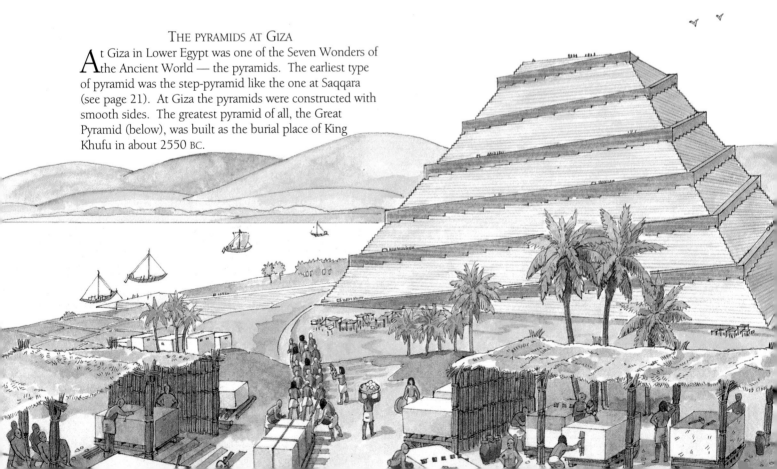

c. 1000 Phoenician alphabet
introduced
c. 800 Maize cultivated in
Mesoamerica
776 First Olympic Games in
Greece
753 Traditional date for the
foundation of Rome
c. 600 Phoenicians sail round
Africa

THEIR ACHIEVEMENTS

Building the pyramids was a tremendous achievement for Egyptian architects, surveyors, engineers and builders. The Great Pyramid at Giza was built with 6.5 million tonnes of stone. Single stone blocks weighed anything from two to 15 tonnes each. Not only did the stones have to be brought to the building site from the quarry, but each had to be cut very accurately indeed. A pyramid's sides were measured to be at an angle of exactly 52 degrees.

490 Persian invasion
defeated by the Greeks
c. 300 Early Mayan period begins
221 China united by First
Emperor Ch'in Shih
Huang-ti
214 Great Wall of China begun
55 First Roman invasion of
Britain

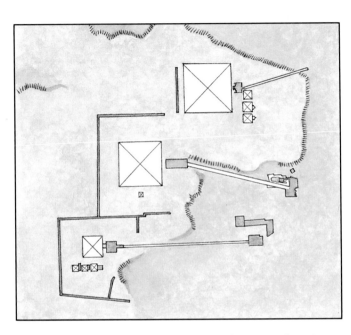

A plan of the pyramids at Giza (above). The pyramids at Giza as they are today (below).

THE NEXT LIFE

The Egyptians believed that people lived after death in the kingdom of the god Osiris. This kingdom was like a perfect Egypt. The Egyptians thought that everyone would still have the same type of life they had when they were alive — the pharaoh would still be king and farm workers would still cultivate the fields.

MUMMIFICATION

The Egyptians perfected the art of preserving bodies after death. This is called mummification (above). Organs like the lungs and **intestines** were removed and kept in containers called canopic jars (left). The body was then **embalmed** by packing it in a salt called natron for about 40 days. Finally, it was wrapped in bandages and put inside at least one coffin.

23

THE LAND OF ISRAEL

BC
c. 1250	Israelites living in Canaan
1020	Hebrew tribes unite
	Saul anointed king
1000	King David anointed
	Capital at Hebron
	Defeat of Philistines and
	kingdom expanded
	The Ark of the Covenant is
	brought to Jerusalem
960	David dies
960–	Solomon, David's son,
22	becomes king
	Great Temple to Yahweh
	built in Jerusalem

587	Jerusalem captured by the Babylonians
333	Palestine part of Alexander the Great's empire
164	Judas Maccabaeus reconquers Jerusalem from the Seleucids
63	Romans conquer Jerusalem

AD
4	Jesus Christ born
29	Jesus Christ crucified
70	Revolt against the Romans, Jerusalem taken and Solomon's Temple burned

TYRE
Tyre was an important Phoenician settlement on the coast of Lebanon during the time of King David.

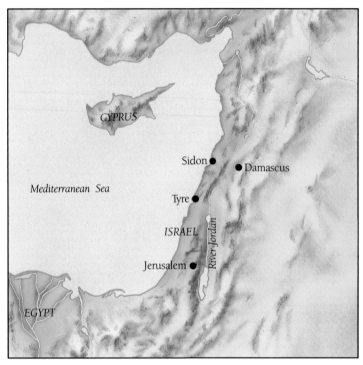

CYPRUS

Mediterranean Sea

Sidon ● ● Damascus

Tyre ●

ISRAEL

River Jordan

Jerusalem ●

EGYPT

SIDON
Like Tyre, Sidon was an important trading town in Phoenicia. There is an Egyptian record which shows that 50 ships did business from Sidon alone.

DAMASCUS
Damascus is the capital of modern-day Syria. It was noted as a trading city in Egyptian records around 330 BC. The town was conquered by the **Aramaeans** and then the Israelites but it was still an important trading city in Roman (in the first century BC) and **Muslim** times (in the seventh century AD).

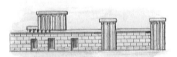

JERUSALEM
Jerusalem was already defended by the **Jebusite** tribe when it was captured by King David around 1000 BC. Jerusalem grew even more powerful under the rule of David's son and successor, Solomon, from around 960 BC.

The Israelites were originally several different Hebrew tribes who began to move into the area shown on the map above, from around 1250 BC. About 50 years later, 12 tribes following the religion of Judaism formed a league against their enemies. The Philistines were one of their enemies who had settled in the south and gave their name to the land called Palestine. At first the Israelites had no overall king but each tribe had its own ruler. Around 1020 BC the Israelites decided to elect Saul from the tribe of Benjamin as their king. When Saul fell from favour the shepherd David was made king in around 1000 BC.

The lands of the tribes of Judah, Hebron and Israel were all united under King David. David defeated the Israelites' enemies and Israel became a great power.

BC

- c. 1200 Hittite Empire collapses
- c. 1000 Long-distance trade by peoples in Australia
- c. 800 Zapotec people produce the first writing in the Americas
- 509 Last Etruscan king thrown out of Rome
- 508 Democratic government in Athens
- c. 300 Mayan writing developed

THEIR LEGACIES

*The most important thing the Israelites left the world was their religion. Their god was called Yahweh. The Bible records an early leader, **Moses**, leading his people out of the slavery they suffered in Egypt. He also took the Ten Commandments from Yahweh which established the western custom of working for six days followed by a holy day of rest. The ideas in the Ten Commandments form a major part of the way many people behave today.*

- 214 Great Wall of China begun
- 100 North Vietnam ruled by the Chinese
- 30 Egypt made a Roman province

AD

- 24 Han Dynasty re-established in China
- 79 Vesuvius erupts, Pompeii and Herculaneum destroyed

EVIDENCE IN DOCUMENTS

We have a great deal of evidence about the people of Israel from documents — some from other peoples like the Egyptians and the Assyrians. But we also have their own writings, mainly the *Old Testament* of the *Bible*. The names of their kings and **prophets** are there for us to read.

SOLOMON'S TEMPLE

King Solomon built an elaborate temple (below) to Yahweh (God) in the capital of Jerusalem. The Ark of the Covenant was kept inside the temple. This area, the 'Holy of the Holies' was only entered once a year by the high priest. The temple was destroyed when the Romans captured Jerusalem in AD 70.

Some of the most extraordinary pieces of evidence found are the documents we call the *Dead Sea Scrolls* (above). In 1947 a shepherd stumbled across several documents in a cave in modern-day Jordan. They turned out to be the remains of the earliest hand-written books of the *Bible*, written during the life of Christ.

THE IVORY GUARDIANS

An important part of Israelite worship was the Ark of the Covenant which **symbolized** the presence of God in the temple. You can see the two guardians standing on either side of the chest, or Ark, which contained the laws given to Moses by God.

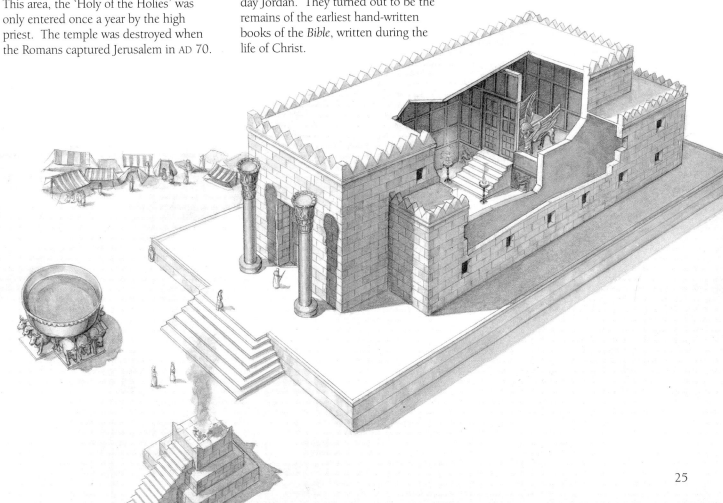

ISLAM

AD	
570	Muhammad born in Mecca
610	Muhammad begins to hear messages from God
613	Muhammad begins preaching in Mecca
c. 630	Most of Arabia converted to Islam
632	Muhammad dies
636	Muslim forces defeat Byzantine army and take control of Syria

643	Muslims overcome the Persian Empire
711	Muslims occupy Spain
732	Muslims defeated by the Franks at Poitiers
762	Capital of Muslim Empire moved to Baghdad
786–809	Reign of Caliph Harun al-Rashid. Muslim Empire begins to break up

By the sixth century, four of the world's most important religions had been founded — Christianity, Judaism, Hinduism and Buddhism. A new religion, called Islam, which was to create a new empire in the Middle East and the Mediterranean area, was founded by Muhammad in 610 in Mecca. Muhammad became a merchant and, after hearing messages from God, began to preach his religion, called Islam which means 'submitting to God'.

The Arab Muslims then began to spread their religion and empire further. They moved west into Egypt and north Africa and north and east, taking over Syria, defeating Byzantine forces, and taking over the Persian Empire. Muslim armies also occupied parts of Spain and north-west India. They even defeated a Chinese army in 751. In 1453 Muslim amies occupied Constantinople and put an end to the Byzantine Empire.

Viking ships like these (above) sailed along rivers to Russia and were carried overland to trade with the Byzantine and Islamic Empires.

Muslim astronomers imported this instrument, called an astrolabe, which was invented by the ancient Greek scientist, Hipparchus. Muslim seafarers used the astrolabe to measure their position against the position of the sun or stars. This one (above) was made in the ninth century AD.

NAVIGATION AND TRADE

As the Islamic Empire grew, new markets for goods were created. Each town had a *souk*, or street market. Traders from far-off lands brought their goods here to sell or exchange. Cities such as Damascus and Baghdad became rich because of trade. By 750 the Muslims controlled all the trade between the Red Sea and China.

Goods were transported by two main methods — land or sea. Merchants travelling on overland routes were well supplied by by *caravanserais* — road stations providing food and shelter for **caravans**. Merchants travelled by sea in dhows to northern Europe, the Black Sea, the Far East and east Africa.

All sorts of goods were **imported** and **exported**. The Muslims produced a range of luxury goods in wood, metal, glass, tile, ceramics and textiles. In return, they imported slaves, gold and ivory from Africa, furs from the **Baltic** and spices and ceramics from the Far East.

PATTERNS

Muslim artists were forbidden by their religion to create pictures of any living creature — people or animals. Instead they used an amazing range of patterns and shapes which were carved or painted (above).

MOSQUES

All Muslim towns have buildings called mosques which are used for worship and study. Each mosque has a courtyard and a covered hall for prayer. There is also a *mihrab*, which is a niche in the wall showing the direction of Mecca. Worshippers are called to prayer at set times of day from tall towers.

THE WORLD

THEIR LEGACIES

In some modern-day non-Islamic countries, such as Spain and Portugal, you can still see the influence of Islamic architecture and art. Throughout the centuries, Muslims have been famous for their learning and inventions. There is a ninth-century Muslim library at Cordoba, in Spain, which contains half a million books. Muslim scientists made advances in medicine, algebra and mathematics, astronomy and navigation. The counting system we use today in the West was given to us by Muslim mathematicians.

MEDINA

Muhammad met a lot of opposition to his religion in Mecca so he set up a Muslim community in Medina.

JERUSALEM

The mosque shown above is the Dome of the Rock, built by AD 699 in Jerusalem. It was from here that Muslims believe Muhammad rose up to heaven.

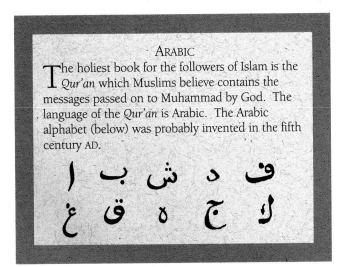

ARABIC

The holiest book for the followers of Islam is the *Qur'an* which Muslims believe contains the messages passed on to Muhammad by God. The language of the *Qur'an* is Arabic. The Arabic alphabet (below) was probably invented in the fifth century AD.

ا ب ش د ف
ك ج ه ق غ

MECCA

Mecca was a sacred place for Arabs even before Muhammad's time. Muhammad and his followers upset the rich merchants of Mecca who were worried that their wealth would disappear if people did not visit the holy shrine there.

BAGHDAD

Baghdad was founded by Arabs and was always full of foreign visitors. The caliph (ruler) built the city in a circle and by 814 it was the world's largest city.

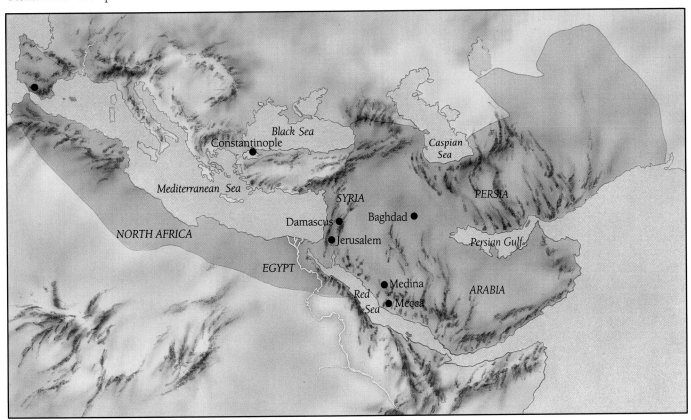

27

GLOSSARY

A

administrators: people who are employed to manage the business of an individual, a company or a country.

allegiance: to promise loyalty to a more powerful nation.

Aramaeans: the people of ancient Syria. The Aramaean language was spoken throughout the Persian Empire.

archaeologist: someone who studies the past by scientifically examining the remains of the past.

Assyrians: people who lived in northern Mesopotamia. The Assyrian Empire stretched from Egypt to the Persian Gulf in the seventh to the eighth centuries BC.

B

Baltic, the: the name of the countries near the Baltic Sea — such as Poland, Denmark, Finland and Norway.

C

caravans: the name given to groups of merchants in Asia and Africa who travel across deserts with their goods carried by camels.

civil servants: people who run the civil service. The civil service is the organization that runs a government.

courier: another name for an official messenger.

cultivate: to tend the land in order to grow crops.

E

embalmed: something, such as a body, which has been preserved by drying and treatment with chemicals.

excavate: to find and dig up an item from the past.

export: to sell goods to another country.

F

fertile: land that can grow many crops is fertile.

flax: a plant with blue flowers, grown for its seeds.

H

hectare: an area of 10,000 square metres.

Herodotus: (c. 484–424 BC) a Greek historian who wrote about many aspects of Greek life.

hunter-gatherers: people who hunt and gather food rather than **cultivate** land or breed animals.

I

import: to buy goods produced in another country.

intestines: the tube inside the human body which connects the stomach to the anus.

irrigate: to water land with small canals or ditches which carry water from a source such as a river.

J

Jebusite: a tribe in Israel which occupied Jerusalem before King David captured it in 1000 BC.

L

Latin: the language of the ancient Romans. Latin was used as the language of learning in medieval Europe.

M

mausoleum: a large and grand tomb.

mercenary: a soldier who fights for any cause or any country as long as he or she is paid.

Moses: the leader of the Israelites in the *Old Testament* of the *Bible*. Moses led the Israelites out of slavery in Egypt and brought them to the Promised Land.

Muslim: followers of the religion of Islam. Islam was founded by the **Prophet** Muhammad in 622 AD in Arabia.

N

nomadic: people who travel from place to place in search of food for themselves and their cattle.

Nubia: a wealthy ancient kingdom of northeast Africa.

nutrients: minerals absorbed by the roots of plants as foods which help growth.

P

pith: the area between the rind or covering of a fruit or plant and the fruit itself.

prophet: a person whom a god speaks through, or someone who communicates knowledge about a religion.

S

sacred: an object or building that is thought of as holy because of its connection with a religion or a god.

scarab beetle: a type of beetle used to represent the Egyptian sun god.

Seven Wonders of the Ancient World: the seven man-made monuments thought to be the 'wonders of the world' by ancient and medieval scholars.

survey: to study land or people in great detail.

symbolize: usually an object which stands for another , more important object, or for an idea.

V

Valley of the Kings: the burial grounds of the pharaohs.

INDEX